Redstart

Contemporary North American Poetry Series

Series Editors Alan Golding, Lynn Keller, and Adalaide Morris

REDSTART

An Ecological Poetics

FORREST GANDER *and* JOHN KINSELLA

UNIVERSITY OF IOWA PRESS
Iowa City

UNIVERSITY OF IOWA PRESS, IOWA CITY 52242

Copyright © 2012 by the University of Iowa Press

www.uiowapress.org

Printed in the United States of America

DESIGN BY TERESA W. WINGFIELD

The University of Iowa Press is a member of Green Press Initiative and is committed to preserving natural resources.

Printed on Glatfelter Natures Book (30% post consumer waste), an acid-free and permanent recycled paper certified under the exacting standards of the Forest Stewardship Council (FSC), whose goal is to promote environmentally responsible, socially beneficial, and economically viable management of the world's forests.

LIBRARY OF CONGRESS CATALOGING-IN-PUBLICATION DATA

Gander, Forrest, 1956–
Redstart: an ecological poetics / Forrest Gander and John Kinsella.
p. cm.—(Contemporary North American poetry series)
ISBN-13: 978-1-60938-119-6, ISBN-10: 1-60938-119-X (pbk)
ISBN-13: 978-1-60938-137-0, ISBN-10: 1-60938-137-8 (ebook)
I. Kinsella, John, 1963– II. Title.
PS3557.A47R43 2012
811'.54—dc23 2012007450

Contents

Why does "the land" have to give something back to the writer? Why do we need to imagine, manufacture, or "experience" some kind of bridge between self and "wild" to give purpose to writing the land?

A history that precedes me. A cultural and natural history that I intuit only partially. Nevertheless, it educates my senses, even my sense of formal possibilities.

This disease of Western subjectivity—this defense of the natural world because it has so much to give us, grant us, return to us, reward us, or affirm us—is the final sliver of aesthetics that would guarantee the hobbling and dilution of any poetic resistance to the killing of the land itself.

Metamorphosed from mica-rich shale, a billion-year-old spine of schist runs from Henry Hudson Bridge to Battery Park in New York City. Where it dips around Washington Square, it has filled in with glacial till, which makes that area a bad bet for anchoring skyscrapers.

But it is hypocrisy to use indigenous knowledge, to co-opt it, as a way of affirming one's own connection to the place that one has directly or indirectly helped oust indigenous people/s from anyway. This is not to say that one can't or shouldn't refer to indigenous knowledges, that they won't necessarily become a positive part of a nonindigenous discourse, but rather that so often it's a veneer of connection and respect hijacked to validate one's own presence and disturbance of land.

What we encounter are translations of our own fables of anguish, ardor, and asseveration. But these translations take place only through obliteration of the originals. Thus the agony in our postures. Bodies breaking under the weight of epiphany.

I should state clearly now that this is not contesting the "I," that old lyrically challenged chestnut, as the "I" is always hidden away there by varying degrees of separation. Nor is it a contestation with writing the self when experiencing the world around us; rather it is the use of the super validated self as "authority," as "reliable" configurer of experience.

It's curious to think that often the greatest degree of diversity, innovation, and hybridity takes place at the beginning, before the codification of stereotype. Rather than genially synthesizing diversely authoritative approaches, hybridity often precedes standardization and the values it authorizes. The hybrid I.

However, I should state that I believe the "I" should always be under pressure: under pressure in what constitutes the self and under pressure in how it operates as messenger and witness.

Beyond my interlocutor's face, there is a scrim of trees and beyond that a forest and hills. Beyond my interlocutor's face, there is a massive building, a line of taxis, and children in Halloween costumes.

Where is the thickness of that perceptual experience on the page? What we acknowledge: *that* is the only ground we stand on.

The destruction of habitat will stop only when people give up on the idea of getting something back.

Poems obviously don't make anyone better, more deeply human, whatever that might mean, more capacious of empathy, intellect, intuition, psychological nuance; poems don't articulate emotional experience or frame concepts in ways that have made any discernible difference to the world—our whiffled clod of suffering and greed same as it ever was—except in one endlessly iterated particular case called, in various languages by various individuals, my own.

Poems for me are disturbed and even damaging. They are about resistance and induce troubling self-criticism. When they fail in this and become a gloss of "experiencing nature," they are joining the big lie

. . . whether lived, visited, or imagined.

The writer communing with nature can so often mean the death of nature.

A crayfish chimney and the female in berry.

For me, writing of "nature," especially in poetry, should be about the carnage to which its production necessarily contributes. Such awareness surely helps us use the poem as a means of resistance, a nonviolent confrontation with the limitations of self in dealing with the crisis so many of us have constituted . . . ?

So the *not-yet* and the *becoming* appear in each other as reciprocal reflection.

JK & FG

Redstart

The Future of the Past

FOR BRENDA HILLMAN AND FOR SUSAN BERNSTEIN

The earth under our feet—We are not asked
to begin nowhere. —GEORGE OPPEN

Better than ever able to trawl through proliferating voices and dialects, we're still aware that the language practices commandeering world history are increasingly standardized, utilitarian, and transcriptional. If we're experts at navigating sound bites, we're prey to clichés and ready-made phrases. With text-messaging, grammar- and spell-check programs, we're offered, in the middle of making a word or sentence, a range of choices for completing it. Those choices are programmed to the most likely conventions. The full range is shoehorned into high-probability solutions. The shortcuts are useful of course, and god knows I can use the spelling help, but they nevertheless nudge us toward predetermined expressions that circumscribe thinking and condition perception.

As globalization draws us together and industrialization and human population pressures take their toll on natural habitats, as species of plants and animals flicker and are snuffed from the earth, it may be worthwhile to ask whether an ethnocentric view of human beings as a species independent from others underpins our exploitation of natural resources and sets into motion dire consequences.

What we've perpetrated on our environment has certainly affected a poet's means and material. But can poetry be ecological? Can it display or be invested with values that acknowledge the economy of interrelationship between human and nonhuman realms? Aside from issues of theme and reference, how might syntax, line break, or the shape of the poem on the page express an ecological ethics? If our perceptual experience is mostly palimpsestic or endlessly juxtaposed and fragmented; if events rarely have discreet beginnings or endings but only layers, duration, and transitions; if natural processes are already altered by and responsive to human observation, how does poetry register the complex interdependency that draws us into a dialogue with the world?

There are, of course, long traditions of the pastoral, poetry centered on nature or landscape, in both Eastern and Western language literature. I, myself, am less interested in "nature poetry"—where nature features as theme—than in poetry that investigates—both thematically and formally—the relationship between nature and culture, language and perception.

I wouldn't propose any particular aesthetic synthesis that embodies the union of linguistic meaning and phenomenal reality. *Compost* seems to me no more a model of nature than *geometrical symmetry* (the housefly's eye) or strict mathematical progression (*the Fibonacci number sequence*). It depends upon how we want to metaphorize nature (which we can't, in any case, ever extricate ourselves from: "Nature is on the inside," says Cézanne to Gasquet). Nor can any definition of the ecological be authoritative. A strict Petrarchan sonnet might as readily suggest to a reader the rigid imposition of authorial control as the humbling sublimation of a writer's choices to a larger (because conventional) expressive pattern.

Just now, the United States and China are locked in a tug of war to determine which country can spew more carbon. For both, natural resources are snorted up for immediate highs. Perhaps these facts place particular responsibilities on the poets of both countries. Maybe the development of environmental literacy, by which I mean a capacity for reading connections between the environment and its inhabitants, can be promoted by poetic literacy; maybe poetic literacy will be deepened through environmental literacy.

Poetry doesn't simply supplement the rational intellect but provides inherent and sometimes incommensurable forms of insight. Because its meanings are neither quantitative nor verifiable, poetry may offer different, subtler, and more complex expressions than the language of information and commerce. An ecological poetry might even . . .

FG

The Carboniferous and Ecopoetics

I

In one of the beginnings, below the fluff- and leaf-encrusted surface of a wide, shallow body of water, microscopic spores swirl with bat-winged algae. A cloudy soup of exertions and excretions, the sea drizzles its grit into rich mud.

Trilobites are dying off. (Miles Davis could have been quoting nature when he said, "I listen to what I can leave out.") Brachiopods, mollusks, and corals cluster in wide, shallow seas riven by sharks. Thick fish with lungs and lobes are giving way to a new species, the lung reconfigured as a swim bladder. Like surreal, underwater candelabra, crinoids effloresce; on long branching stems they stretch up toward the waves, each arm filtering small animals and plants through the calyx where a mouth is hidden.

Aquatic insects begin leaping from the water to escape fish. In some, the gill plates take on the quality of wings. (*Donde una puerta se cierra, otra se abre*, Cervantes writes: where one door closes, another opens.) The Carboniferous gives rise to six-winged insects. They need compound eyes for navigation. There are bugs that would look ordinary to us, and there are giants, huge mayflies and predatory dragonflies with thirty-inch wingspans. They hover over bouquet-size spiders and a sort of millipede that grows five feet long.

Because there are no flowers, the insects are plant suckers and spore feeders; they eat seeds still unprotected by fruit, and they eat each other. They live in burrow holes and on the forest floor, and they colonize tree crowns. They jump, crawl, and soar into and out of the canopy.

Below, in the umbratile interval between one step and another, a tetrapod resembling a large newt freezes and blinks into the sound of the world, the chirp and whirr of insects and the high frequency mutter of its own species. Fronds brush fronds in a light breeze. (And what, eons later, does the Kreutzer Sonata, which Tolstoy will deem dangerous for its capacity to arouse erotic feelings, what does that music have over this sound?) The animal blinks again, its hydraulic limbs holding it above smudged tracks that mark where others of its kind mated, their mouths popping, cheek muscles bulging. Five tumescent digits on each foot channel ground vibrations into neural impulses. It takes stock and goes on. ("I am still alive then. That may come in useful," Beckett's Molloy quips.)

The air is rich with the smell of chlorophyll; oxygen levels are spiked. There are no flowers, no pollens, no vivid plant colors. There are no grasses, but vegetation is beginning to climb slopes, reducing runoff and erosion. The first mosses have appeared.

Conifers and tree ferns fifty feet high tower over swamps of horse-tails. Because temperature and humidity hold steady, the trees rise so quickly they lack clear growth rings. Ferns luxuriate across wetlands: dragonfly seed ferns, rhizomatic ferns, ferns spoked like the dorsal fin of a swordfish, each loosing into the air millions of spores coated with oil and chlorophyll. Every plant on earth releasing oxygen, but taking carbon with it to its grave.

In the Carboniferous, the graves are considerable. At the end of their life cycles, plants topple into the water and mud and loam. They accumulate so quickly, they don't have time to decay. Branches, seeds, leaves, and debris fall into pools already thick with aquatic plants and algal blooms. The buried mass goes brown and peaty under an ever-increasing load.

Beneath hundreds of thousands of meters of overlying rot, the peat beds contract like a frog's iris into thin, horizontal lines. Water, oxygen, and hydrogen are pressed out. The organics harden into lignite. While the swampy basin continues to subside, heat and intensifying pressure metamorphose the lignite into soft coal. (And "*the darkness is white, but not / white like the white that existed / when . . . trees existed*," writes Inger Christensen.) Spheroidal masses of minerals like calcite and fool's gold bind and clot in the seams.

(The Romans pass along a word, *conticinium*, for the nighttime hour when the world goes quiet. The Carboniferous collapses into a night that goes quiet for 300 million years. When we pick up a piece of coal, it is the fossil residue of photosynthesis, a condensation of Paleozoic sunlight that we hold in our hands.)

As soon as humans enter the picture, the story speeds up. Four thousand years ago, the Welch ignite funeral pyres with coal. In 1673,

8

two Frenchmen document coal beds in Illinois. But not until the nineteenth-century industrial revolution is coal assiduously mined. Shafts are drilled into coal seams; rooms, pillared with timber, are excavated. In dusty lamplight, miners break down the coal-face with a hand auger, a pickax, and blasting powder. In every cubic meter of air they breathe, four to eight billion dust particles circulate. Once a day, the fire boss comes through with a safety light and checks for gas.

From before the Civil War to the mid-twentieth century, men separate coal from shale and rock binder, and they shovel the coal into loading cars by hand. Billions of tons are heaved and cleared from mines by human muscle. Chinese workers arrive in the U.S. and help lay rails for coal-fired locomotives. Jimmie Rodgers records "The Singing Brakeman."

At full throttle, technologies advance: undercutting machines, roof bolting, ventilation, mechanized loading, conveyor systems, strip mining, and then, about three decades ago, mountaintop removal mining. In West Virginia alone, more than 350,000 acres of forested mountains are lopped off, and 1,200 miles of streams are buried. The overburden or leftover rock fills adjacent valleys. One of the by-products of excavation is slurry, a pool of chemical waste and toxic metals. Postexcavation by-products like ash and poisonous gases are released in the next phase: the burning of coal in power plants.

Because most coal contains pyrite (ferrous sulfide), combustion releases sulfur gas. Sulfur dioxide, nitrous oxide, and mercury, all toxic, plume into the air. And so, of course, does carbon dioxide. Isotopic fingerprinting of carbon in the atmosphere links it directly to the burning of fossil fuels. Coal is the dirtiest fossil fuel, producing twice as much carbon dioxide as natural gas. CO_2 in the air, its density increasing 200 times faster than ever before, captures reflected heat and holds it to the face of the planet like a pillow. Meanwhile, some of the sulfur dioxide precipitates out of the skies as acid rain; the mercury finds its way to the ocean.

By the end of the twenty-first century, a mere three hundred years after coal was first intensively mined, a vast amount of the carbon that accumulated underground for over three hundred million years will have been released into the atmosphere. The relation between those two sets of numbers, three hundred and three hundred million, represents six orders of magnitude.

In the United States, power consumption from coal will probably rise almost 2 percent per year through 2030, faster than energy consumption from petroleum and natural gas combined. There are over 400 coal-fired plants in the United States and at least 114 more plants under construction. In China, where more than 6,000 men died in mines in 2004, where coal seams in the north hiss in unstoppable fires started by small-scale mining operators, and where the deserts are yawning wider at an alarming rate, coal is powering unprecedented industrialization. Some scientists estimate that coal will provide half the world's energy by the year 2100. And a hundred years after that, all the exploitable reserves of coal in the earth with be exhausted.

———

A poem, even excavated from its context and the time of its writing, is a curiously renewable form of energy. It's hard to be sure whether it is from the future or the past that the poet Henry Vaughan writes: "They are all gone into the world of light! / And I alone sit ling'ring here."

FG

II

The term ecopoetics has taken on a wide range of connotations. Among them: a variable set of technical and conceptual strategies for writing during a time of ecological crisis. These strategies (which look a lot like innovative poetic strategies championed for the last hundred years) often make claims to initiating

1. a dispersal of ego-centered agency;

2. a stance of self-reflexivity (so that, for instance, it is said that the poem originates not within the self but within the landscape to which it is given back);

3. a rejection, as Australian poet Stuart Cooke writes,[1] of any attempt to "gather the world into some kind of unity and permanence" in favor of an "encounter" with the world marked by "entropic fluctuations" (ecopoetic texts are sometimes described as "open texts");

4. a rigorous attention to patterning;

5. a reorientation of objectivity toward intersubjectivity.

To bolster this last intention, ecopoetics has been linked to studies in neurology. While the attempt to reinterpret objectivity as intersubjectivity goes back at least to the nineteenth century, to Franz Brentano and Edmund Husserl, the contemporary neurologist Antonio Damasio helps provide a science for it with research that suggests that "consciousness consists of constructing knowledge about two facts: that the organism is involved in relating to some object and that the object in the relation is causing a change in the organism."[2]

The world, Damasio implies, is actively involved in our perception of it. The phenomenologist Maurice Merleau-Ponty made the point earlier when he suggested that the tree *offers itself* to our vision. In most ecophilosophies, traditional Western assumptions about the distinction between the controlling subject and serviceable object are reassessed. The ego-logical is redrafted as the eco-logical.

So eco-logic (as Félix Guattari claims in *The Three Ecologies*) is not focused on binaries; it isn't dialectical. Instead, it means to question "the whole of subjectivity" and rethink the self as "a collective singularity." As the poet/philosopher Richard Deming puts it, "To suggest there is a subjectivity to which 'self' refers is not necessarily to hold that, as such, an 'I' must be a continuity."[3]

It isn't a radically new idea to consider that the *I* is multiple (since Nietzsche and Emily Dickinson both say as much) or that the self is interconnected with other things and beings (as animists believe and as Edmund Husserl and Brenda Hillman propose). But the founder of deep ecology, Arne Naess, extends the idea into his call for a worldwide and unimpeded "self-realization" for all subjects, human and nonhuman.

That's a call that leaves me on the porch smoking with Bobby Bland, "two steps from the blues." Because *that call* is awfully hard to make. And maybe, in any case, we should be looking to make a different kind of call.

Félix Guattari prods us to learn to see ourselves as a collective singularity, to "construct and in a permanent way re-construct this collectivity in a multivalent liberation project. Not in reference to a directing ideology, but within the articulations of the Real."[4]

Some of the questions we might ask: Who becomes responsible for separating the Real from ideology? Does that attempt lead us back to a notion of prelinguistic, primordial reality unstructured by language? Is there a way to perceive the Real transparently, without depending on deeply problematic translations of the world into word? Is there any foundational reality apart from our constitutive and perspectival translation of it?

Many of the descriptions of the relation between poetry and ecology are metaphorical, and the metaphors have been thoroughly mixed. A poem expressing a concern for ecology might be structured as compost, it might be developed rhizomatically, it might be described as a nest, a collectivity. Its structure might be cyclical, indeterminate, or strictly patterned. The formal possibilities are as infinite as ever since there isn't any formal structure for representing ecology or nature. And writing is a constructed system.

Looking back for a moment at deep ecologist Arne Naess's imagination of "self-realization" for all subjects, human and nonhuman, we are faced with another nagging question: how can our perception of nonhuman indications of "self-realization" be unimpeded by our interpretations? While it's true that many cultures—the Pirahã, the Navajo, Australian aborigines—may experience relatively more transparent relations with "the spirit world," there are still inherent translation problems.

And who determines, and by what criteria, that one poem "issues from the land" while another poem "issues from the self"? Who validates certain poetic techniques, approaches, forms as a priori ecologically ethical or unethical (as William Carlos Williams once called the sonnet a "fascist form")?

It's interesting to consider classical Chinese poetry, which—with its absence of personal pronouns, simultaneous but nonhierarchical meanings, indeterminate term relations, and linkages between the natural world and the world of human emotion, perception, and experience—satisfies many ecopoetical aims. Yet the Chinese have a long pervasive history of what the Western world calls animal abuse and environmental degradation, not to mention a deeply hierarchical social structure and oppressive political regimes.

Maybe there is no reason to expect that values purportedly connected to poetic form encourage behaviors structured by those values. Which is to say, maybe poetry makes nothing happen.

In linguistic circles, the Wittgensteinian argument that "the limits of my language mean the limits of my world" is still debated, often couched in attacks on—or variations of—the Sapir-Whorf theory (which proposes that the particularities of a language influence the thought of its speakers). Most ecopoetics are linked to some sense of political urgency and to the belief that language is centrally involved in both thinking and culture, a position calling into question anyone's claim to absolute certitude. It's been suggested that ecopoetries, by offering revised, less dogmatically binary perspectives of interaction between human and nonhuman realms, suggest ways of *being* in the world that might lead to less exploitative and destructive histories.

Two recent studies interest me and, although they aren't dog-in-the-sun proofs, they register support for the argument that language, perception, and conception are irrevocably interconnected. The first is the highly publicized field work of Daniel Everett, who reported, in "Cultural Constraints on Grammar and Cognition in Pirahã"[5] and in two subsequent books, on a Brazilian-Amazonian tribe for whom linguistic communication is restricted to "the immediate experience of the interlocutors." Their language doesn't have a perfect tense. It doesn't allow for the possibility of embedding, putting one phrase or sentence inside another. They have no numbers, no concept of counting more than one, two, and many, no color terms, no abstractions, no myths, and no sense of history going back more than one or two generations. Despite one hundred years of contact with Portuguese-speaking Brazilians, they are monolingual. Because their language does not allow for expressing experience beyond the experience of the speakers, they don't say, when someone in a canoe disappears around the bend of a river, "He is gone from sight"; they say, "He is gone" (from experience).

Another study involves the Aymara of Bolivia. This interests me in particular because I've cotranslated two books by the Bolivian poet Jaime Saenz, whose work is notably influenced by Aymara language and culture. In the Aymara language, it is impossible to say something like "Joan of Arc burned at the stake in 1431," since that sentence is unqualified by anyone's experience and because every sentence must express whether an action or event was personally witnessed or not. According to Rafael Núñez, a cognitive scientist at the University of California, San Diego, Aymara is the only studied culture for which the past is linguistically and conceptually in front of them while the future lies behind them.[6]

To speak of the future, Núñez explains, elderly Aymara thumb or wave back over their shoulder. To reference the past, they make forward sweeping motions with their hands and arms. The main word for eye, front, and sight in Aymara means the past, while the basic word for back or behind also means the future.

It has been suggested that in a culture that privileges a distinction between seen/unseen and known/unknown to the extent that evidential acknowledgments are requisites of the language, perhaps it makes sense to metaphorically place the past in front of you, in your field of view, and the unknown, unknowable future behind your back.

In these cases, there seems to be a close relation between the particu larities of language and the perceptions and conceptions of the speakers of that language.

If language does affect the way we think about being in the world, poetry *can* make something happen. I would suggest that it does. Certainly, I feel it has profoundly influenced the way I experience the world. But it probably doesn't affect perception nearly as directly as poets might wish. Getting rid of the capital I, eliminating pronouns altogether, deconstructing normative syntax, making the word "wordy"—these techniques, all more than a century old, impact the reader. But the effects are complex and subtle and may not correspond to a writer's intentions at all.

Perhaps, instead of modeling ecologies, poems might be seen to take responsibility for certain ways of thinking and writing, as Charles Altieri notes, "precisely by inviting audiences to see what powers they take on as they adapt themselves to how the texts ask to be read."[7]

What if structures of perception are not "subjective" (that is, added by humans to raw data) or "objective" (provided by things in themselves) but are articulated within a media of relation and interaction such that to speak is to surge up into a medium that isn't projected, but is ongoing like an environment? Might we see ourselves then as participants in a noninstrumental language?

Would there be any way to know?

FG

NOTES

1. Stuart Cooke, "Orpheus in the New World: Poetry and Landscape in Australia and Chile," *Antipodes: The North American Journal of Australian Literature* 24, no. 2 (2010): 143–150.
2. Antonio Damasio, *The Feeling of What Happens* (New York: Mariner Books, 2000), 133.
3. Richard Deming, *Listening on All Sides: Toward an Emersonian Ethics of Reading* (Stanford: Stanford University Press, 2008), 9.
4. Félix Guattari, *The Three Ecologies* (London: Continuum, 2008), 86.
5. Daniel Everett, *Current Anthropology* 46, no. 4 (August–October 2005): 622.
6. Rafael Núñez and Eve Sweetser, "With the Future behind Them," *Cognitive Science* 30 (2006): 401–450.
7. Charles Altieri, "Some Problems about Agency in the Theories of Radical Poetics," *Contemporary Literature* 37, no. 2 (1996).

Codex for a Protest

Herewith I provide the hideous background and framework—and in
part only—for condensed concertos of an errant camera

for Forrest Gander

there's no landscape to speak of
strophe

"It is not growing like a tree"
But like a tree it perishes entirely:
Its grey core wheedled by ants and elision,
The distance from here to there constrained by vision:
       A nesting box falls,
       Yellow parrot palls.
    Lines and remembrances have their say,
    All unfastens from surface as they stray.
It's truly the time of the golden whistler,
It dominates light-time, detail's arbiter.

antistrophe

Ants and wolf-spiders long for science,
And they long for fugues with compliance.
Earth-turning lizards poke legs out of the shed,
While shadows from painted wood are decayed:
       Which tools carve this music,
       Compliment a redcap's logic?
    Cosseting the evocative, leave's blankness
    Contretemps: a glossary with few words in use;

Belief stretches our ordinariness, that sacred
Reserve of enjoyment, eternal makeover of the acrid.

epode

Septic, the line of waste that thins to water,
           A width of seepage
That angles as it descends; irony—so little water
           And yet the seepage;
           And yet a wattle glows
           In the socially monstrous
        Epiphany: growth makes splendid the air
           We share with refineries,
           Eponymous adversaries,
       So anything growing here makes repair.
Some giveth, some taketh away. And in between
We mark off days, registering the seen and unseen.

On a foggy morning on a bridge
between two counties between two religions
that left wedding clients in limbo, a celebrant's uncomfortable
joke, amidships the ship's list ready, that runneth over
mountains immediate as sparse flowers floated
through emerald vision: see triggers within hulls,
facemask exactitude of a nuclear weapon: latched onto
memory, Irish migrants on the Thames mixed with the tide,
those patterns of English piano teachers setting out
after husband and father dead on the tracks—
you know that photo of Dharma Ginsberg on the tracks,

plutonium triggers en route? At least sweat drove him

to complicate to sit and make simple his urge, upthrusts

and blue morning flourishes amazed by in-betweens,

thoroughly incantatory and glorious; artwork

school prizes fallen from their shelf: giltbound

Shakespeare and a History of Hitler; between chronologies,

Scottish miners athwart their Presbyterian nomadism

a contradiction to delve deep in the telling, like gold

and sailing, shipwrecked fortunes: that's cargo

and no inheritance: so much traveling, so much

mi-

gration.

          Exsanguinate soil and deeper rock

          seams of glitter to hoist like cloth

          beneath a dinner setting; diesis

          shafts to opportunity, then

          excavated to open pit, richest

          emptiness still receives, its fullness,

          effluvium loved through what hope

          it makes: white goods, bread on the table,

          distance between extremes.

Out of a Fremantle sidestreet across from an ocean

blocked by yachts piled high, a few houses away

from the brothel you knew and that knew you: loud,

agitated and contra; Nina Hagen incited and walls

punched through, hallucinating and cracking up

on Supermen and Ceramic Squares, wondering

why the neighbor's kids strangled their kittens

and your housemate on her bed of five divined

the Seventh Fleet would bucket down hellfire

but could be loved and hated into despair,

betrayal, treason. Ampoules of lovely

morphine becalmed me, lovely doctor,

lovely brother from the Bronx who made love

to the girl I introduced him to, so he'd let us in, let me in,

to open the way into the Harlem Renaissance,

to turn against his white overlords and their big

grey boats. Bookshop workers loaned money

from the till, I cavorted with lesbians under

the wharf and loved them, was arrested

by a schoolmate who made a good officer,

and the Australian Nationalist Movement

attacked us, KILL PUNKS, backed by the rigors

of gleaming bayonets raised gangplank guards of the Fleet,

Australian Secret Service snap happy

the day racists got the backing of all and sundry,

and when I waved to the television camera (those waves,

those waves), my beloved grandfather fell out of his memory:

so make fragments and cadenzas and allusions

to our nineteenth-century purpose, our grand planetary

design: those wanderings, gatherings of images.

It's how you bend your knees
inward when you dance, how you worship
when not a skerrick of your surroundings
is taken into account: some ethereal possibility
or misgiving, some lyric intoned
as the piano keyboard is fully explained
and all that spills forth is majestic and sublime
and full of such gross and penitent
purpose: sound collateral resounds to connect
with an arsenal of lockdown, unprimed warheads,
sheer firepower of God!

As if it were possible for me to explain
  how Couperin stimulates, electrifies my brain:
    so many tests done and they'll know why
      I was always going to die (and did): "Light fragrant,
        manifest . . ." says Thompson, whatever
          punctuation;

what do I in fact
want you to understand, Forrest? It's not a question, you don't need
'em: I don't comprehend or imply the cultish nature
of compadres or compliance: I expect opposite time when
binaries and contraries are neither one nor other with meaning: left
  high

and dry in the lockup, watching a Nyungar kid being tossed

round a circle of cops, eight or nine cops in a medieval ring,

a Fremantle Star Chamber that took slices out of flesh,

and made the land Norman. Wouldn't you repeat yourself,

garble the history to save the facts? Murder, mate, murder.

Witness.

      Damn these lines,

        mucus trails cross

          police cells, vestibule and shitholes,

            heavy cleaners that will cause

           cancer clusters before

            they've a catchall term:

count syllables for clues. Rethink rhythms: leftover particles

    to ring poetry out of: a geology of crust, mantle.

Pulling blood back into a syringe is like marble art at school. See,

    there's still

a place for similes, and the beauty of onanistic backwash is to get

    every

last drop, or less than a drop, that powder already drawn through

    fibers

of a cigarette butt: in that state, your authority to resist the Seventh

    Fleet

is naturally questioned; questioned, naturally. But the rush, the rush!

That "Nativity in Black"!

Rasp after staged event
prescribed and delimited
dun as dust

dun as dust
prescribed and delimited
rasp after staged event.

See, when they arrested me—prior, *a priori*—and took away
drugs and country the latter never asked by me and still despised,
I discovered O terms of lateral empiricism—ghosts feeding
on ghosts inhabiting ghosts taking away any sense of sexual freedom
or intactness, that you *want* to inhabit ghosts in the cells of the dead:
even those who would emigrate cross bodies kill you off
as soon as they see the ocean—for jail, even overnight, is a cave:

"*Ce qu'on entend sur la montagne . . . ,*" as if, per I am left
off-centered sans reference, guilt I store in lymph, reminiscence
of regret so bird-like, so carrion in grain-eaters: note repetition,
NOT conflict of image, please;

it's all my false starts,
all collaboration with high hopes goes nowhere
because it comes out of nowhere, just declines
into specks of its necessity, splashes about, diminishes;

Take the character of my friends
joined as one unit in total pro-
test, a wall against the Fleet sends
a message of defiance, throw
of the dice against an azure
plural sky, it's the dry allure
of opposition that helps them
think strategy, the threads and seams
of flag fodder, enjambment and
welcoming of sailors a-cross
and conquest and sharp orders
sent through brothels and white white sand;
honestly, the lines are no more
than captions for building "terror."

I believe NOTHING and YET behave as if "The Hellhound
    is on my trail" but "can't look back": I dare, I double dare:
lost to us, lost in inserts, in formulas of modernism and nature,
    in excerpts and additions, bon mots, over-readings,
and why would anyone intentionally isolate themselves
    without even the reassurance of anaphora? Of anaphora!
Pray tell, pray:

            rise to no avail
            rise to no avail

and yet, the wedge-tailed eagles are back.

Overhead. Staking the great York gum at the peak
of block.

Strands twist torsion tension, proclivity.

Nest. Nest.

Wedge-taileds once edged the city, sea-eagles the coast, the river. Sud-
    den as,
"Hands up who's interested in vigils held in visions of punk bands?"
    Local,
very local: *King Pig, Thou Gideon* whom you fought over their meat
    fixation,
all those syllables you'd look to arrange as peace but didn't know how:
    punked-out headjob, smack dealers with submachine guns
shooting up their own night clubs. You jumped a roof a roof or two,
    you jumped a roof a roof a roof.

Check deaths in custody, match times, names.
Same names of same "attendants" come up cross genres
and with self-interest, straining against Norfolk pines lining
the beaches, the ballast of a ship-culture, the Roundhouse

beneath which I lived, where I drank and injected

and was beaten. Another way of telling a story

that is anonymous for those others: I can't remember

their names and they were taken away. And the stains

of the East, distant country, where in the Cross I was raped: stains

have their own politics, and mostly aren't forensic. Addicts

don't get raped, addicts don't protest, not really.

Not like they're *actually* going to stop that train,

that gunboat: it's that call of the wild. Rape is hate.

We protest it. Messy of me to mention confusing tenses

which never have anything to do with grammar, but believe me,

and read Georges Simenon if in doubt, everything is to do with

    paragraphs:

the pleasure is all theirs (disambiguate), and Pat Califia

can place a dog collar around her own fictions.

            And all this because

            chopped down trees disagree

            with me? That I rabbit on about genetic

            modification, wrestle with technology

            and self-immolate with complicity: burn me

burn me, friends   charred as a jarrah forest. It's a quarter

of a century since I dined on animal: a Tolstoyan sense

of history, trapped in narrative? Gloating

through the Scanner Darkly. I abhor
religion, but don't abhor saying so?

Snap.

But I admire those
with deep religious convictions.

There are hoaxes
worth their airplay, and false prophets worth listening to;

And, you know, all I got from Baudelaire was love of me-life,
El Dorado and Souls. Postpartum.

So, back then, '85, Jack van Tongeren's Australian Nationalist
    Movement,
usually sandbagged in their urban bunker making forays to blow up
Chinese restaurants, beat punks with baseball bats, stickup their
    anti-"gook"
posters, broke the feet of dreadlocked protesters, chanted
    pro-American
but anti-Asian and anti-Black epithets. I asked, but what IS America,

and went *down down down*. The Lord protecteth those who bomb
and maim and murder. Plain simple. Like expressions
and skins not too exposed to the sun. We defaced their flags,
all of them. Still do.

A potted history of anarchism
versus fascism in Fremantle,
Western Australia. The Wobblies and prose poetry. Don't
trust in me, I will resist fascism at every opportunity:
I remain suspicious of closure. I thank their God
that I became pacifist. I truly and holily do.
I can tell you a pacific gull on the Indian ocean
sat high that day on the tower of a destroyer:
the aircraft carrier USS Carl Vinson, nuclear-powered,
sat off Gage Roads. So big, *so very big*.
Nursery-rhyme big. A ferry service
to and fro, back and forth,
All around the world.
All around the world.

No skies carry *all* chapels in negative light?
In the holy breakdown: nanoparticle by nanoparticle: it's how
we clean the dust on the dust of our surface of surfaces.

Ha, Hofmannsthal—

quickfix illumination; read slowly

and lose what precious time you have within fields

of conjunctions and prepositions: lashings of instructions,

bordering always on legalese,

so richly exacting,

awakening.

So: splendour in the light,

comfortable digestion,

sex that works into sleep and beyond,

ability to forego the anti-nature

of food and gold through plants

you recognize from childhood—an increasingly distant

childhood—facsimile stories, fairytales, myths?

Maybe snaps whose coloring can't quite be made right

even with newish software.

We were all whiz kids once.

And now, naturalists, we see red birds about the island.

Laura Riding was deleted in the syllable count.

She married prose.

We invest too much hope in good chemical feelings

called relief.

A balance of the earth's plates

anywhere

at any given time?

Stations measuring, waiting.

We are measurers. Adding up. Subtracting.

Repetition is a trap, our deaths.

New histories bend epics

and tragedies and arrangements of aphorisms (policy, not polity):

and so I imagine a museum in which we all walk on the same side, all

going to exhibitions from which we won't return;

bereft of nature I rant and rail against excess
but equally damn the middle path: it's an ex-addict's
disquisition of adrenaline, a propelling
of new routes to congress, a disappearing
of adventurous aviators;

try buying nothing other than food, for a month. NOTHING,
nothing at all. Rest on no pillars, sleep in no towns, spread
where no stars blanket your yearnings. Traffic in God.

For, in part, I have moved on: still
cradled in the Avon Valley: interpolated
wheat:

> Frumentaceous, as loquacious
> as harvest brag, though light-on
> yields heavy drought taxes, re-
> payments crippling, and bird
> namings make little difference.
> Never wanted the mystery.

> Far east crushing floods.

> Since moving on, partial
> as roadmap page-turner
> revealing different districts,

coordinates point you all over
the leaves, electricity still
pouring in, expanding light
to vanquish emptiness?

No, wear night as skin,
your skin expanding,
pachyderm. Body, a globe.
As water gathers, crack
in great tank, white
feathering. Honeyeaters
drink sunwater.

Frumentaceous, lateral
lop to horizon chaff
expulsions. Each seed
coated. Added skins.

Still in Ballardong Nyungar territory,
still beholden to a mythos of the seven towns
of the path to burning salvation:

Brookton

Beverley

York

Northam

Goomalling

Toodyay

New Norcia—place of the monks and broadacre farming decorated
  with almost ancient olive trees

all the way to the Spanish monks and their presses, artifacts, stone

    oven

breads, stories of their stories; overtelling others' stories: that where

    we

fit in, I and *I*: to implicate *you*

at some point of the drillcore,

turning at such high speed—bit that cuts

with no water to cool

its descent: refrain

in refrain, clause

by clause, phrase on phrase: a morphology

of distractions and acute desires

to name, collect, hoard.

It's real estate, and the landhounds, here,

are ripsnorters:

        New estate developer fixates
        agency reports back to component
        geologies, out-turning inner earth,
        recycled toxins to concentrate,
        pro-rata dictate extricate relocate
        offensive industry in high definition,
        acronymic soil cleave to air, skylight.

        When buildings depart a city
        it loses ordnance but ceases
        municipality? It's what we wonder

in country, rural census and worse job figures.

I could always go back to work the tractor.

Ownership; buzz; title-deed hustings
hiss to coat seed up-and-about periscope
lunge as lungful; storms of Venues, rich
clouds of boiling overtures, less
strokes of mighty tractors, land-
breakers skidding scalds and waves
of colloidal light: *light*, light, quality
lifestyle to bring desired change,
spending power in realms of food.

Take no souvenirs.

No curios.

Our visible needs.

JK

A Note on Ecopoetics

I have grave doubts that an "ecopoetics" can be anything but per-
sonal. I have grave doubts ecology can be anything but personal. And
a luxury that few have. I feel that "ecos" should be communal, but
individual selfishness regarding the use and abuse of "environments"
means a default to individual culpability. It's cumulative but can be
broken down to individual agency. Maybe not individual choice—in
fact, outside wealthier countries, much less so—but certainly individ-
ual presence. But poets operate in communities, and their ecologies
are crosshatched. They connect and divide communities that aren't
even aware of their existence. A poem is a part of an ecology—it uses,
and maybe gives. I've always found collaboration a way of challeng-
ing the security of self-affirmation. Of recognizing the crosshatched
nature of an ecology. Of creating a field of failings and inadequacies
and announcing common purpose in trying to repair and redeem.
Collaborative writing can be redemptive.

This writing is a map of my conditions out of which arose a series of
poems exchanged with a fellow poet. A fellow poet who is concerned
about damage done to ecologies and interested in the "nature" of
exchanges about landscape and place, like myself. Maybe we feel a
kinship and a compulsion to exchange texts. To connect and diverge.

In reaching a desire to record one's own coordinates in a damaged
ecology, an ecology trying to cope, I realize how much of the data of
background is contrary to any idea of "nature." There's some grim

stuff in there. Most of our own biographies have grim stuff. Place is about event as much as location. Place is interstice. Place is also a reckoning of intrusion and damage and the labeling of forces (greed, "security," self and communal empowerment, spiritual materialism) that seem adverse to the health of a biodiversity. And so this schematic diagram of what informs residues and remnants of old-growth ecologies, of farmed landscapes, of points of contact with the organic and inorganic nonhuman. The human drive for narrative is never far away. And it's the narrative I'm—we're?—wrestling with.

JK

Redstart

Flash-in-the-pan scene stealer,

prowling and scanning dry-grassed

bank of red dirt and granite knuckles,

attention seeker, spotlight grabber

as sun busts through atmosphere's

protective layers, thermonuclear fashion show,

trees on the hill dead as water dips below

distance roots might reach, called

down to zero where pull is drop

on subterranean survey—hey, hey, rustle

in grass, sleek bungarra, sand monitor,

long-necked, open-chested prancer,

swatching with adhesive tongue, tail sweeping: goanna,

totem, prinker, barely scutellate, lunulate spots

to grasp as soothsay or dog-in-the-manger,

to hunt against silence: start or startle,

race across the flats, leap to lower ground,

the bank made to stop land falling away,

rough as guts to offset your rarefied

hunting, lip, sip, and suck,

soured on creatures retreating

where water once flowed.

JK

Where the ear

cocked

rivertoward

registers silt (and

leachate) scouring

boulders, water's

oracular

interior, quartz clatter

at edge and breaks

(brecciated)

cataracts of whirled

[indecipherable], gusting

rain, ripple-drifts

across swirl over

swallet hole

where plastic

bottles trail a skiff:

current, sun, thrush,

retina. Kingfisher

swoops (in-

seminating gesture) as

we "in our porous skins"

continuous with,

indistinguishable

from—

FG

Ha! Like the Indian and Southern oceans

in their crosscurrent slapdash exfoliant grinding

meet, their chop and change, undertow and underdrag,

stone testament and rack-and-pinion wrestling

of the eddies and flurries, waterwheels

and propellers, screws and sails

twirled to windsocks, they tack the flow

out to the straight and narrow, tickle

hatches of periwinkles, trawl

beaks of barnacles. By the river today,

the Swan choking on algal boom, nutrient

double dip, city's cistern,

down from inland, up from sea mouth,

memory and out-of-body wiring

take me there—that's south of here,

a couple of hundred miles, south

to where the oceans meet, where waves

pluck pink out of porphyry

                                        J K

. . . escarpment,

micro-plutonic,

and early Cenozoic. Glacial

in its naked. Stop.

Red zones on the climate map

"proliferating." Cockroaches

coast the restaurant wall. Stop.

A woman at the back table lifts

her hair to the other shoulder. Stop.

86 on walrus-heart soup.

Men's room closed, sewage pipe

clogged by a glove. You

need to go outside. Stop. There,

where a flock of herring gulls

walks from the stormy beach

across the country club

golf course. Leaving

the performance. Glow-

ering responsive light. Stop. Stop.

Porphyry cobbles in

driveway. Pink

going red.

FG

Red plumes red, dust red, reddened

claws of black eagles, red scores,

red contours in flesh of wallaby . . . out there

we wandered, wandering kids away

from home, kids away from mothering,

listening to the slam dunk

of bolt-actions; we wrestled

red in red dust, wrestled until the flocks

got the better of us, entrapped as sandstone,

layered in dry red river beds, wind gutting

phantom water; our little escapades,

mini tales of wander: scratched

and scarred by hakeas, scratched

and scarred by bluster; listen, listen to the ore trucks

rolling in from desert, ripping roads,

shifting on their axles: bravado bluster bravado bluster; dust a carpet,

ringing echoes of the crushers, ball mill fantasias,

as delicate as red-tailed black cockatoos

landing, so immense, so trailing

bloody windows, to worship outdoors

in scoured flatlands. We lift and lift

to follow straggling sheep, lift in single file

behind them, behind their reddish leader, straight to where water

might pool, where water might be

still.

J K

At the edge of a benevolence

by means of affiliation. And   held up

        there   in an experience given

multiple entries like hatches

of periwinkles. Or   given a "moment's pause

    with the color of it,"   but still

insensible to the signature

    changes that fling us

        into an assertion   of

   ourselves   in a garden lettered

with birds.   Some yellow-shouldered

  grosbeaks   pish-in real well.   A flicker

          in its starring role as   flicker

hiccups over the continuous

world. As the waiter (what is   at stake?) places

    a dish of garlic-olive   oil

on the soiled tablecloth,

        we return to ourselves,

fog   ladled   onto a beach.

  On our plates, black   Bolivian

   potato cakes. And

       were we arguing about what?

  with warm plantains

at arm's reach.

              FG

I hear that bird afar, I hear re-

play

clash a surface: plash

and echo,

ripples dusty

sketchlines

wavering coolants;

first fog of colder season:

can't occlude them, can't offset

such purpose. Who believes

a waver: striving in botanics

to make large trees grow larger,

shilly shally in shady corridors,

exercise all verdure?

Bellow mezzo, below a pleasure:

laterite I bother up-earthing, catch a flow

of blue-green algae,

sheep right down and out—"country" / "rurality"—

at the river, nibbling at the killer

salty water,

thin as fog is think,

constitutive

occult: where any water comes from?

But I breathe a feather,

a weighty

drift of egret flung wounded

across rezonings:

city, semi-urban, semi-rural,

  "country"

JK

. . . where she

stands, over

mingled odors of her

watering can

and the white

narcissus. Mammal

and flower,

soil, water,

hair. Her sweat-

drenched shirt clings,

transparentized

there. And in the

humid air,

a garden

spider, head-down,

finds web

center. What

might not be

measured out between

desiccated and

astir? Before

petals release

their allure

and night turns—

FG

Fish or flesh? It washes down the grid

to flow a distance out to sea: some

never go that far, just stay inside

the scarp, across the hills.

Fish or flesh? Plurals

set as tandem ploughs, close-set disks,

doubling furrows to medical edge:

small swimmers—little fresh water

to capture here,

barely fish. We rub our flesh

to make ends meet.

A name comes naturally,

and then you see: theory:

searching traction in the muddy soil,

dust a day ago, dust again,

shortly. Ghostings:

the keepings out, the wallings in: clusters

of stone, wood, drainage. Shout out: SOUTH,

they're small enough to call "28s,"

here—"CENTRALLY"—"ring-necked parrots."

slightly different species:

south a name we might add up, multiply;

an editor says: asks: "what you bangin' on about?"

Hey, rumption in the wattle,

soliform the blossoms: yellow ring

encircling both; this poetomachia

cullers would have us play

when growth is sparse

and none will share,

the wedding day

away away.

JK

Scuffed out	glyphs on	sand-
stone	birds	drain from sky
high	intensity trucklights	blinding
what	lives in darkness	eyes
turn inward	Despoblado	returns
to flower rain	sotol	ocotillo flame
come first	kangaroo rats	to creosote bush
sage scent	piñon	the visible
intensifies	hawk blazing	in branches
down logs	and snags	a Neolithic
sun bites	into rock fly	maggot sucking the
black ant's brain	irreproducible	conjunctions
release the	redstart's	trilled song of

F G

Somebody told me what jazz was and I jump-
startled, took heel and twisted, jigged
in my resolve to elucidate, variegate:

and smothered cock-a-hoop as pinned,
I shot out from the grip: lancet bedazzled
so hung-up on light I bubbled

like paint in too much heat: it's the wet
that's come! The wet! The wet! The plenty of rain.
Drought buster; birds clustering

so deep, so broad in the beam, feathers
on doorsteps, around tree bases
feathering scrub-like-talons.

Scan the plains, scan the hills
rain sick   rain weary
green black with volume

plump hearts filled to burst
trill   abrade   reshape

JK

muddy boots

lined up inside

the barn door

cows miserable

in the lee

of the hill

it's all I do

now he said—

I suppose

he didn't

hear me—

holding the bucket

in one hand

stripping tit

with the other—

and I know each

one by its humid

eye—the ground

outside plopping

it's deafening—say

what? say—cow

cocking an ear—

the rain's

falling pretty

healthy it

stinks like

heaven in here

FG

Time passed in portions
  to anneal a movement
    out, about, resplendent

as elegant parrots: that's where
  I've been showing,
    display and hearsay,

chatter, gossip, some details
  accrued by others: capillary
    eviscerated   conformed

as schist if geologist would say so
  or not. I did know the kestrel,
    struck by its strike

apnoea hover: so burnt, so much closer
  to sun, popped through
    protective layer;

soulful collusive, collecting
  without objects: Benthamite
    rumors take what

away from here, to gather,
  archive, where I walk changes,
    degrades worse for wear;

how ruffled the overly colorful

  curved-beaked rainbow

    bee-eater: out

of its burrow, a photo

  not taken, collection

    or gift of site.

                 JK

Phased and tilted,

    a philanthropy

of tunnels and saliva, soil

      particle gripping

soil particle: heed the hollowing,

      heed the high climbing, a building

wingspan from mucilaginous

      bodies, legs "just special

effects": how affected

      and pernicious all scriptures

and hymns.

FG

Hellshines

  lonely and birdless, I mean,

rain of feathers and claw and beak,

  no space to ululate,

no causative to rest

  laurels of eremophila

ensconced in aridity;

  where mulga parrot

betters a gaping lyric,

  where limit is talk-about,

all censorship of subject;

  never outlook, nor winnow

seed from dust, splore

  of separatist joy

that so worries husk, nub,

  embodied tongue.

JK

Unsprung the

crab-spider rushes

self returning to itself

over the lip of hibiscus

petal all detail

and anticipatory

to bite the bumblebee at

the nape of its pollen-speckled

black neck subject and

event so suddenly conjoined

the stinger pulses in

my finger: no mercy

but frankness which makes

now visible and gives

it durance clods of jetted

soil clump in

ploughed troughs

against crabbed and

broken stalks

where I walk

my breath one

rhythm among

others I am

depleted and desolate

in the autistic twilight

self returning to obsessive

self dog to its vomit.

FG

I do self too, in self-same split
of bark: what emerges takes the bite
out of my harp, relinquishes
a rash of leaps and trills;

the heat upstarts by eating down
into dry parts, and flaked out
on the mattress, we—believe
it or not—sweat;

Self is a to-do here: a clicking bird
I can never find when I creep below
the canopy, when I hold back
steps that break the brittle

twig's rickety spine; share code,
code share, village of the damned:
skinks on brickwork
so much older

than childhood plans; spare
in the lair, I concatenate: listen,
bust a boiler, water cooling
as it falls from burst bolls

high high overhead where antonyms
don't count and tiny eggs are laid
by beetles and not birds
that click.

JK

The rain has stopped (almost stopped) and

from helicopters the corpses are invisible

(almost invisible) the potholed road hellshine

and migrant children playing

with medical waste (floating) under a bridge

while behind them in the city hived

from spectacular greeds a migratory warbler

(yellow-throated?) leaves its ghost-print

on the double-pane glass of the tower and drops

(eleven stories) if I'm not mistaken

this month is April hence the rain (almost

stopped) and a strange receptivity to despair

so his mother says (in his presence)

she does not hate her son nor does she

love him whose father (unknown) forced himself

on her (his one beastly face among others)

left alone while her three brothers drove their

lyre-horned cattle across the savanna (the heat

upstarts) under circling vultures

F G

I went out this evening

with my daughter who has a pressure

in her head and needed the quiet

of the river, just flowing

from recent rains. In the late sun

spot fires in paddocks venting

their tension, she insisted.

I said: it's about the light,

Katherine, the sun filtered

through, swallows scything

and seemingly unaffected.

But they are. And the river

can move though appear stock-still,

reflections compiling,

as if rolled over one another.

The swallows are sharp here as well.

Upriver it shallows

and the water thins. They get less

rain there even when fronts

look inland. Surface structure.

Perceptual strategies.

And other factors.

JK

SEEDTAUT

Emplexed germinal, rushed
    to fray the sticky soil,
its nodules: fractual leavetake,
    tri and quad, coaxial:
listen to the deadlines, listed
    sane and fricative,
furrows and furore; staunch
    as planter that random
pegging: sap creative, sap ooze
    prompting bark raptor, blotting
footer, prayer-making. And
    none no why, none claim
to know why: plants with reddest
breasts, birds will burnished leaves.

                         JK

LITTORAL ZONE 19 (FOR MICHAEL FLOMEN)

Mobbed phosphorescence, gaseous swarm upon which (impossibly) watermarks are stamped, rings clinging to invisible membrane, discrete, unrelated to the (lower) dimension of volcanic tuff, stone sponge.

But though we have no criterion for how to see and are not sure what we are seeing, we are plunged into sensation. As into a novel pain. Though saying so yields no shred of information.

Impact marks
throng the resin.
Declension: a focal
spasm the lid
releases. Nocturnal
pods, invertebrate and
membranous, surge
in a phantasmic
standoff. Unsodden
bloom: inversion
puddles hissing
against the scorch
of annunciation.

FG

RIPSNORTER

On the lookout for, a landgrab,

plot to nurture, a ripsnorter

where nature flexes, burrows:

that living thing, to guardian

& protection, richer or poorer,

running water *optional*, wishing

roots deep to hang in there,

bush that beats that weird,

    that eerily grotesque,

    breakaway that rarests

       orchids.

                JK

Seeing property divvied

    along title lines,

surveyors rejigging

road access, zoned

    rural residential,

but the price soaring,

and left, alas, hang-dogged,

    hung-out-to-dry,

    gazumped

in realtor apotheosis: "winter creek"

the sluice through salt scalds,

    "lifestyle change"

    the green mist

percolating from neighboring farms:

amid the action, picking

    through ram horns

and tines and drum after drum;

but then, last week, the flags

    rose in town

and none could unpick

their meanings, like being

    bogged down

in dust, being rural and land-caring.

                     JK

Incident, Evidence, Conclusions

Thud	Lights on the hill	Vehicle
Abrupt departure	Red aftermath	Abort or vanquished
Crescent moon	Discomfort	Shadows shadow
Crash underfoot	Leap of dark	Roos in paddock
Torchlit wetness	Blood or urine	Pisstanks or killers
Systems analysis	Desire for order?	Abandon all hope
Injury and escape?	Sleepy hollow renamed	Jam Tree Gully

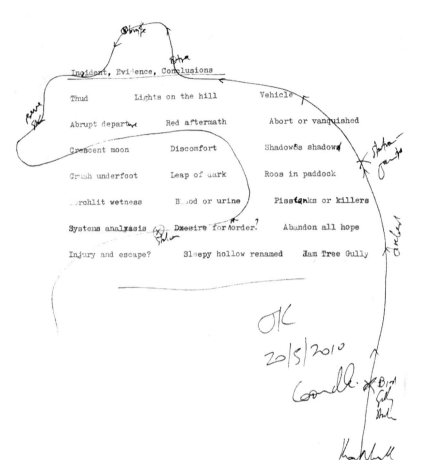

The Movements of Yellow-Rumped Thornbills: Twittering Machines

1

Today I watched the resident yellow-rumped thornbills cross the road at the top of our block and make for the lone tree sitting in an eleven-acre paddock that crowns the granite hill. It's the first time in sixteen months I've seen the group (a more appropriate term than flock, but maybe I should say "community" or "cell") cross that road. Their habitual route is usually framed by the neighbor's eight acres below us, our six acres, and a small portion—maybe four acres—of the sixty acres of reserve that abuts "our" western boundary. Their seemingly carefully timed visits (or, maybe, "stations") around the area have always been patterned, with the odd member of the group flying off at a tangent, but rapidly returning. The route is basically circuitous and, though altering slightly or stifled by weather conditions, seems to persist beyond the lifespan of any individual weather, with aberrations really present only during nesting season. I have timed the composition of an entire book of poetry by their movements. The thornbills, tiny birds that they are (not much bigger than the smallest Australian bird, also resident here and often joining the thornbills in their flocks, the "weebill"), sing loud and in concert, and with a deeply informed dialogics. Their conversations shape the conversations of the human presence on this small piece of land we are attempting to "restore" over time, in the context of drought, earlier fire damage (before our time), and other "trials and tribulations" of our "presence."

When we moved here permanently at the end of 2009, we'd had a year of observing the thornbills on a regular basis, during "visits" or "excursions" from our old place some seventy-five kilometers away near York. Thornbills were there as well, and though I had observed their movements, I had been less able to get a sense of their range. There, it seemed to be greater and to extend out into the bush in a way that I couldn't measure. Here, at Jam Tree Gully, in this very tight and focused valley, it seems more immediate and particular to a narrower band. And in the spirit of a positive pathetic fallacy, I bend this to my poetics because it bends my poetics to itself.

2

I am picking this writing up a couple of months down the track. It has rained very little and it's already mid-May. The yellow-rumped thornbills are extremely active and are "patterning" according to the lack of water—relying on neighboring troughs and leakage from pumps and windmills that aren't governed—the irony of green patches in the dry. The waste, and the necessary opportunism of creatures.

I have been watching the group of thornbills intensely. They have changed their range and route to incorporate new water sources. But it's not proportional expansion of territory, moving like an echo, rather like a bubble, an aberration in the circuit—a diversion at a tangent that then returns to the protracted space of their interaction. Weebills often join the thornbills' group, though they seem to have their own variations on the route: dipping in and out to form their own "weebill groups," then rejoining the yellow-rumped thornbills.

One other change in the route is notable. They are following the firebreaks around the block. They even do the "square," kerning the corners but following the sharp angles nonetheless. The acreage is lines and nodal points—especially certain trees: the large York gum up near the top gate, but also the dead tree just over the fence. In the mornings this is an intense hesitation point before they dart across the road onto a neighboring "property," and over the hump of the hill to water troughs on another property, then fast back to the dead tree. It's a distance but takes no more than ten minutes.

The fact that the round trip is so quick might well be for two glaring reasons. Firstly, that it is an aberration due to water issues—an experimentation come about by a vanguard bird that discovered or located the new source, returned with the information, and established a temporary subroutine for the others. Secondly, that the block over the road is eleven acres of dry grass with little tree-cover. And in the one big tree at the crest of the hill, a pair of black-shouldered kites often roost and would easily pick off thornbills watering at a trough. So, caution in terms of safety but also caution in terms of pattern. It is not hard to transcribe this into issues of innovation in prosody, nor into Bachelardian "desire lines." But that's too easy, as these lines are restive in ways I have not yet been able to "unpick."

So much is deceptive about these little birds. Their song is often described as "tinkling" or "musical" and even "cheery." They are also generally considered to be more "solitary" birds than many others, though they "cooperatively breed." But here, on neighboring "properties," and in the reserve next door, they group and fume together in song. They travel in groups that are alive with cross-movement and cross-reference. Their song is "cheery" and volatile. It is fast and slow. Their brilliant yellow-tailed tiny bodies erupt and hide themselves. They are "theatrical" with one another, with me observing them. They work in choruses and soliloquies. They are passerine, a "perching bird," that internally migrates from perch to perch of one tree, then from tree (a gathering of potential perches, potential linguistic "branches") to tree. Their lexicons and etymologies are fixed but able to grow as well. I have heard and noted this. Labeled in colonial terms by the French in 1830 (at King George Sound, according to Wikipedia), their species part of their scientific name (*Acanthiza chrysorrhoa*) comes from the Greek (chryso—"golden"). And, indeed, their poetry is like that of Greek "*dekapentasyllavos*" poetry. I have counted fifteen syllables that seem, to me, rarely "twittering"! I will wind Paul Klee's "Twittering Machine" as irony in the poem. Another aspect of transcription in terms of a poetics and a correspondence (literal and figurative).

The weebills (*Smicrornis brevirostris*) that accompany them have a song that complements and counterpoints the thornbills' chatter. Some say it is a "wee-bill" sound (weebills have tiny bills, and the name relates to this); others describe it as a "wee willy wee-tee," but it sounds "zweet zwit" to me. They cross-talk the thornbills, and maybe in sharing knowledge of a route and variations, they talk cross-species. I'd like to think so. A shared "property" or properties of language. Familiar collocations?

I seem to work the movements of the yellow-rumped thornbills into not only poems but letters to people. My communications become

diagrams not so much of their dance movements, but of their aggre-
gations and digressions. When I spot a variation, I feel a need to tell
somebody. A grounding or questioning of the unified self?

And regarding this vanity of identification ("I" assimilate to "them,"
and in turn become part of their mimicry—as with magpies and ter-
ritory, the acceptance of the person walking the same route each day,
the dog barking at the same time as I wrote to someone today—or at
least part of their patterning of space), I note that when the thornbills
stop in the tree on their stations opposite the window where I type,
they now put on a dramatic display and approach the window. I see
them seeing me, and vice versa. They puff up their tiny chests and
flutter around. I am not trying to ironize or diminish their chests in
describing this (an appalling missionary condescension) but to cre-
ate a visual for the careless noninvested observer. It would seem that
way. Somehow I have either been accepted or included; or maybe it's
a rejection, their own affirmation or statement of resistance against
surveillance. Which is the flaw of all science: the subject rejecting the
observer and corrupting data and resulting conclusions.

3

It worries me that poets want schematic diagrams to fit their poems
to. A template poet, I no longer want templates. Influences, yes—the
thornbills and their patterns influence me—but I don't wait to mimic
or ape their stratagems or, in that exclusive and bigoted take, their
instincts. I do not recognize the instinctive. Cumulative knowledge
that is a priori is not writ in the blood, but writ in the length of time

it takes to judge choice. The infinitesimal gap between events means less time to make that choice. Survival relies on avoidance of procrastination, but that does not mean choices are not being made, even if they don't transcribe into consciousness. My views are changing as I watch the thornbills, as I write this essay.

4

An event last night has reconfirmed how doubtful I am of poetic "practice." Of systems. Of means of tracking meaning. That the best poems are simply forms of intellectual, aesthetic, or emotional (or any combination of the three) Sudoku. Poems, no matter how haphazard on the page or in casting distance between associations, ultimately demand a mathematical solution. Evasiveness, the reader filling in the blanks, the torment of allusiveness, all in the end beg for attention, for social and personal affirmation. Distrust the chorus as much as the solo.

An event last night: about 7:30 PM. Dark, crescent moon, stars full-bright. Hear a car pull over at the top of the drive. Look through the window and see it right near our front gate. That's about 200 meters away. It sits there. I watch it and eventually it roars off. I go up in the darkness, up the steep winding gravel drive. I hear kangaroos in the paddock to my right, they move and stop. I head back to the house for a torch. Back up the drive I hear the kangaroos move again. I go through the gate and shine the torch around. There's a large wet patch in the middle of the road. It's not blood. I fear a kangaroo has been struck yet see no real evidence, but I still hear and see vague, dark shapes of roos in the paddock.

This morning, early: walk up to see Tim off to the school bus. The wet patch has gone, evaporated, even in the cool, moist air. I see a skid mark on the roadside and some scraping marks—could be a roo or boots/shoes. Someone stopped and walked around the car and pissed on the road? One pissed on the passenger's side and another on the driver's side? They hit or targeted a roo and it hopped off over the fence into the paddock, injured?

I search the block for an injured roo but see nothing, other than two newly dead trees from the long dry. One is a forty-foot-high York gum. The thornbills are emerging from "Bird Gully," as Tim, our seven-year-old, calls the lowest point of the block. Where I have walked to check the evidence cuts across the flight paths of the thornbills. They avoid that open paddock area where the roos were last night, but do follow the firebreaks. Not at night, though—they roost in silence, with the odd cheep if disturbed, ruffling themselves then settling back to rest. Whatever happened last night was in their range, their daily purview. I wonder if it will alter their patterns, at least temporarily—if they are affected by "bad vibes" or a spiritual uncertainty. Something not being quite right—as it must necessarily affect the way I shape a poem or think about approaching a poem. Even the most consistent pattern I am aware of in the world around me is vulnerable, and I can't shore up my certainties with the false patterns of prosody.

5

I haven't noticed any fighting among the group of thornbills (nor between the thornbills and the weebills contesting for insects and larvae), though I find it hard to account for the variation in their numbers. Sometimes the group is about eight birds, sometimes fourteen or fifteen, allowing for the subgroup of weebills. Are they two groups of thornbills overlapping and interacting or a number of groups who share nodal points, crossovers as in a Venn diagram? Gisela Kaplan, in her classic study *Australian Magpie* (Melbourne: CSIRO, 2004), follows Robert Carrick's five territorial subdivisions for magpies. The final of these concerns "permanent territories." Of these she notes:

> Establishing a territory can be very hard work, requiring continuous vigilance to defend and maintain it. There may well be a different set of problems in the center of a territory as against the fringe of it (the center-edge effect) and the territory may never be secure from being taken over by intruders. Magpies who own permanent territories have the highest stakes and most to lose, and so will need to be vigilant all of the time. (35)

Of course, there is little or no behavioral correlation to be made between thornbills and magpies, though both share insects as part of their diet (and thornbills will eat seeds, of which there are plenty on the block at different times of the year). However, magpie territories certainly overlay thornbill territories here, though clearly the magpies have factored the thornbills into their territorial picture as a nonthreat. They are, after all, very small, and even in groups seem to offer no threat to them.

I have made a specific point of minimizing my textual investigation of the habits of thornbills for this piece, as I want only what's observed to inform the poetics of recording. That's like creating a poem with no knowledge of prosody. And that's the key: obviously one takes a certain amount of comparative knowledge to the process, but by limiting it, one limits prejudices of form. Form is imprisonment, though some form can be liberating. Magpies fight with other magpies to defend their territory, but I have witnessed no conflict between the thornbills. I have seen them upset with other birds, certainly as nesting time approaches, and I have seen them almost "gang up" on larger birds, but in general their energies seem spent on food collecting, communication, sentinel activity, and a vigorous display and response during courtship. But that's my limited way of seeing, of course. In the future, maybe I should concentrate on observing their interactions with (or ignorings of) the weebills. Their sharings and disputes. Their mutual aid. The messy nesters (thornbills) versus the neat nesters (weebills—they weave a dome-shaped nest).

The key to creating the thornbill poem is the center-edge effect: the search for a central theme, the opening, middle, end approach, the retention of solid lines and shape throughout a stanzaic, metrical, and rhymed poem would attempt to thwart perceived weaknesses at the edges, when in fact there is both no more weakness at the edge and no greater strength in the center. Even using prosodic "devices," I instill enough "errors" to default to "open form." Substitution in metrics, slant rhyme, and slippage in meaning encapsulate this fluidity, but still recognize the geographical (and attendant social and political) differences between what is perceived as the center and what is perceived as the edge. The magpie from outside the territory trying to encroach will meet most resistance at the center; that's logical. I must be wary of imposing my own pacifist desires on the thornbills. Their center is mid-territory (where the group might never fly) or mid–the group? That's what I need to consider and also in terms of the shaping of the poem.

With regard to magpies, Kaplan continues: "One of the disadvantages of territoriality is the constant need for fighting or vigilance flying, activities that require constant high-energy output, higher than perhaps required in a semi-nomadic or highly nomadic lifestyle" (35).

Accepting that one could challenge this in so many ways—"nomadism" brings its own energy outputs—it seems logical that one might carry this generalization across to the obviously territorial thornbills. But clearly working as a single community on the one hand, the varying number of the group and possible shift in membership when nodal points with other groups are met, seems to suggest on the other hand a nomadic territorialism: a dyadic communalism. In the poem, this is both marginalia and eclogue: a song competition in which victors and losers exchange places. Ritualized but without dire consequences?

6

A cold, crisp start to the day. First day in a week that there hasn't been a morning fog filling the valley. I went out looking for the thornbills, "strategically" placing myself near the top paddock of the block where they cross from a clutch of jam trees to a single jam tree next to a firebreak, then inevitably follow the firebreak at right angles to their next stop near the top gate. As the days have shortened, the thornbills are emerging later. I hear them down in "Bird Gully," but they don't emerge. Instead, a pair of male red-capped robins are fighting it out for "access" to a group of female red-capped robins (who don't have red caps), who in turn are themselves agitated with each other. The kerfuffle might have something to do with the thornbills' reticence to start their movements.

At the moment I am rereading Proudhon's *What Is Property?* (edited by Kelley and Smith, Cambridge: CUP, 1994). I am reminded, "From the distinction between possession and property arise two sorts of rights: the right in a thing (*jus in re*) is the right by which I may reclaim the property which I have acquired, in whatever hands I find it, and the right to a thing (*jus ad rem*), which gives me a claim to become a proprietor." With this in mind, I would highlight Proudhon's response to these distinctions:

> In writing this memoir against property I bring an *action pétitoire* against all of society. I prove that those who do not possess today are proprietors by the same title as those who do possess; but instead of inferring from this that property should be shared by all, I demand, as a measure of general security, its entire abolition. (36)

Though in the strictest sense, the bank can currently sell this block if we don't meet the repayments—we own in terms of our names being on the title, but have mortgaged to the bank—we will, in another twenty-five years, technically "own" the place in terms of Australian property law (generally having come out of British Common Law, although "registered title" is Australian). Property law in France at Proudhon's time arose out of Roman Law (Civil Law), manifested in the Declaration of Rights, then the Code Napoléon (Article 544). Of course, the law of private ownership in Australia does not include airspace, nor what's below the ground, so governments (and through them private companies) can, for example, mine minerals for their own gain (and less the governments' and people's gain!) or force purchase or reclamation of land for government projects. It always bemuses me that poets writing colonial-derived "landscape poetry" in Australia don't write with more of an awareness about the conditions of "place" they are observing and interacting with.

I reject "property" in all its forms. I only ever refer to this place as a "property" with scare quotes and irony in mind. It is land stolen from the Ballardong Nyungar people, whose relationship with land was and is custodial as well as spiritual, religious, communal, totemic, and interactive. It is also, to my mind, land to be shared: between not only people, but plants and animals and people. We see ourselves as custodians under a corrupt system that would damage it more than we do and would offer fewer rights to animals and plants than we do. It's a relationship of necessity, not of choice.

In observing the thornbills delay their forays due to the activities of other birds with their own patterns and needs, I am reminded of these issues of possession and property because, though each clearly states an act of possession in the territory they move through, they (willingly or unwillingly—I have no idea) seem to accept a shared proprietorship over their "zone," as well as mutual possession. The

terms of that possession shift due to social and environmental cir-
cumstances, but the sense of "property" remains. For me, this is why
any poem will have to remain open ended, resisting not only closure
but also "opening." The narrative is too dependent on coordinates I
am not privileged to understand. I think the key is in these words of
Proudhon's: "The right of occupancy is equal for all" (66).[1]

There is clearly a problem with cultural and ritualistic specificity
(spiritual as well): that location is identified with the totemic and a
specific relationship with place and that "equality" is often subjugation
of minorities, so one has to temper such statements with the real-
ity of conditions. So too should the poem be tempered: a poem that
merely represents and instructs is going to "miss" the articulation of
rights we all have as individuals (as do all living things) of place, with
community, with ecologies, and also with the "unseen" qualities of a
given space (spiritual, mystical, phenomenological). The system of the
thornbills' movements suggests, more than anything, a rejection of
systems in poems. The thornbills will return to their patterns, but are
willing to adjust to the conditions and to the "needs" of other species.

7

Nesting season doesn't usually start until July. That's just over a
month away. But the thornbills are behaving "oddly," or "unusually."
That's more of a comment about my own tensions of observation, in
relying on their repetitions and patterns, on their scanning the block
with as few substitutions as possible. I have grown to rely on them;

I adjust my day and writing accordingly. But they are fractious and busy and altering their flight paths. They make dome-shaped nests with a false entry. The area is rich with building materials: twigs, bark, leaves, grasses, and moss. I have a good idea where they are preparing to nest down in "Bird Gully" and across at the reserve, but I do not want to intrude, and won't. I will steer clear of those areas unless I have specific "property" needs to go there (erosion problems if we get a major downpour, the appearance of deadly nightshade, which I remove by hand to prevent the shire wanting to spray). It doesn't need to be my "property" for me to follow these self-imposed guidelines.

So, in a few months there will be nestlings to feed, and to collect food, parents will make flights that take place outside the larger group's general routine but that are also encoded as subroutines across the cycle/s of their lives, having already altered with egg-sitting duties. Older birds will probably "vanish" (from my purview and comprehension) and patterns will no doubt change or be augmented. There will be deaths: birds of prey, weather, old age or sickness, cats, and humans. I suspect that the hard shell of movement and behavior will stay similar unless something definitive or catastrophic takes place. Fire, storms, agricultural activities in the district, aggression from humans "attacking" the reserve land. I will, no doubt, embark on yet another poetics, wait until another template presents itself for a prosody and purpose for writing poetry, or until I search it out.

JK

NOTE

1. The notion of property is the issue that burns below the surface of all I write about this place. Proudhon is only halfway there with "Property is theft!" He fails to investigate the nature of such theft: that's more the key to understanding the implications of surveying, gifting, selling, claiming.

A Note on the Collaborative Process

From early 2007, when the first "installment" of our collaboration
was launched with the permission to "feel free to do as you will
with the above, f—or not; continue on, reject, rewrite, meld, what-
ever . . . ," we worked intermittently until late 2009 on the poems
that we eventually titled *Redstart*, a dialogue between possible
"languages of place" (principally the Avon Valley in Wheatbelt and
the "central west" of Australia and Rhode Island, Virginia, and the
Chihuahua Desert of the United States and Mexico).

FG: Please tell me what you are up to. Your own notes are as close to
the vest as detective dialogue.

JK: 4.18am - i think i have an idea beginning for a reply. it rests in
pacing/s and spaces. in the s/pacing/s. hmmm . . .

FG: sorry that my poem is so different and not in keeping with what
i've been doing. it's just that after yours i felt the need to shift
things, f.

JK: the poem is intense and necessary. it cannot be "replied" to but
a response will come back, from this place. which connects with
"that" place as well. a complex subtonal conversation.

JK: okay re mine, f— though of the three parts, "phased and tilted" originally came at the end after "hellshine." but it works okay the other way as well so leave as is, i reckon! just sent a new section.

JK: i've also thought about the essay. though i have one almost completed i think i'd like to take the stuff i wrote you in that long poem framework ("codex") that was part of the original exchange and re-arrange it into prose-poem justified blocks and set out as an "essay" with a few additional chunks (on fire). would that work from your point of view?

FG: That's just the kind of essay that most interests me these days, John. Sounds exciting. I'm over here heading from Madrid book fair to Barcelona today, feeling oddly unlinked from what I recognize as my life.

JK: back to ya tomorrow—been outback.

FG: I love your projected title, *Redstart.* Love what you did with the introductory essay, your avoidance of any sort of academic or logically determined sentencing in favor of a subjective and all the more incisive and dazzling (and historical) syntactical flocking. Like a tornado of dicksissels rising out of a field.

JK: 4.17 in the morning here. i will now retire for a couple of hours and contemplate the spaces between words and see what replies! thanks.

FG: Sweet John, The triplet bungarra lizards arrived yesterday!

JK: i've attached the original lyrical version of the codex poem i wrote for you. i have separated off the original prose statement i made that was part 1 (short) of the revised "essay" version of the codex. i'd like to use that re opening our "joint" intro. you can take or leave what you want from it, but it's where i'd like to start if possible. i will also email a few "random points" for potential absorption into a whole.

JK: it seems, to me, that this could really have something to say, really do something. i'd prefer to stay off the literal web as much as possible but am happy to swap emails via tracy's address (and good old fashioned dial-up out here in the bush) to complete this work. so as attachments? it really helped seeing it in printout form. i am inspired all over again! next stage is an essay from me? i will write something fresh over this coming week. something about kangaroos and "here" and "there" and projections into the worldspace.

FG: Hi John, I'm in Japan now. Japan just put 2 billion into a world biodiversity fund. The U.S. as ever stalling. It's funny writing to you and seeing Tracy in the To: box—a bit like these male Noh actors in female masks, with beautifully feminine hand gestures.

Acknowledgments

Stanzas from "Redstart" beginning "Where the ear" and ". . . escarpment, / micro-plutonic" and "At the edge of a benevolence" appeared in *Dublin Poetry Review* (September 2010).

The prose sections beginning "Better than ever able to trawl" and "The term eco-poetics has taken on a wide range of connotations" appeared in the *Chicago Review* 56: 2/3 (Fall 2011).

"The Future of the Past" appeared in *EcoPoetics* 06/07 (2006–2009).

"The Movements of Yellow-Rumped Thornbills: Twittering Machines" was published in *Poetry Review* 100: 3 (Autumn 2010).

Two of the fragments on "Codex for a Protest" are extracted from unpublished sections of *Graphology*, a "life work" in progress.

Thanks to the University of Western Australia, where John Kinsella holds a professorial research fellowship.

Contemporary North American Poetry Series